DR. BOB'S
AMAZING WORLD OF
ANIMALS
BLUE WHALES

By Ruth Owen

WINDMILL
BOOKS
New York

Published in 2014 by Windmill Books, An Imprint of Rosen Publishing
29 East 21st Street, New York, NY 10010

Editor for Ruby Tuesday Books Ltd: Mark J. Sachner
US Editor: Joshua Shadowens
Designer: Trudi Webb

Photo Credits: Cover, 1, 4–5, 7, 8–9, 10, 13, 15, 16–17, 19, 20–21, 22–23, 24–25, 26–27, 28–29, 30
© FLPA; 11 © Alamy; 12 © Shutterstock; 18 © Jamie Hall, NOAA.

Library of Congress Cataloging-in-Publication Data

Owen, Ruth, 1967–
 Blue whales / Ruth Owen.
     p. cm. — (Dr. Bob's amazing world of animals)
 Includes index.
 ISBN 978-1-47779-028-1 (library binding) — ISBN 978-1-47779-029-8 (pbk.) —
 ISBN 978-1-47779-030-4 (6-pack)
 1. Blue whale—Juvenile literature. I. Title.
 QL737.C424O94 2014
 599.5'248—dc23
                                    2013035981

Manufactured in the United States of America

CPSIA Compliance Information: Batch #BW14WM: For Further Information contact Windmill Books, New York, New York at 1-866-478-0556

Contents

The Blue Whale

Welcome to my amazing world of animals. Today, we are visiting oceans around the world to find out about the enormous blue whale.

A blue whale

Let's investigate...

Hank's
WOOF OF WISDOM!

Blue whales are the largest animals on Earth. In fact, scientists believe they are the largest creature ever to have lived. They are even bigger than the biggest dinosaurs!

An adult blue whale can grow to be longer than a basketball court.

Blue whales have grayish-blue skin. Some blue whales have a pale grayish-blue skin with a mottled pattern of dark spots. Others have dark skin with pale spots.

A blue whale's enormous tail

A Whale's World

Blue whales live in oceans all over the world. They sometimes swim near coastlines, but mostly they live in deep water away from land.

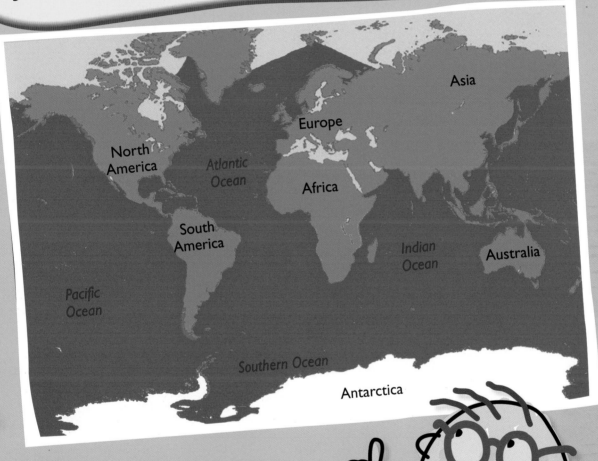

North America

Atlantic Ocean

Europe

Asia

Africa

South America

Indian Ocean

Australia

Pacific Ocean

Southern Ocean

Antarctica

The red areas on the map are where blue whales live.

Scientists still have lots to find out about blue whales. They believe that some blue whales live in one area all the time. Others **migrate** from place to place at different times of year.

Blue whales may move to a new area to find a better supply of food. Females migrate to warm oceans to give birth to their babies.

All About Whales

Blue whales belong to an animal group called **cetaceans**. This group includes whales, dolphins, and porpoises. All cetaceans are **mammals**. They are warm-blooded, give birth to live babies, and must breathe air.

A cetacean breathes by opening and closing a blowhole on top of its head.

A blue whale's blowhole

A blue whale's blowhole is like a giant pair of nostrils. Each hole is so large, a small child could crawl into it!

Most of the time, blue whales swim underwater. They only come to the surface for a few seconds at a time to breathe.

When a blue whale breathes out through its blowhole, water sprays out, too. The water spout can shoot into the air three stories high.

Water spout from blowhole

Blue whale

Blue Whale Bodies

Blue whales have long, **streamlined** bodies that get narrower toward their flukes, or tail.

Head

A blue whale has two flippers on its sides. It also has a small triangular dorsal fin on its back, that is about 12 inches (30 cm) tall.

Flipper

Tail flukes

Blue Whale Size Chart

Dorsal fin

Tail fluke

Flipper

Length = up to 100 feet (30 m)

Weight = up to 150 tons (136 t)

How heavy is 150 tons (136 t)? Each of the groups of things below weighs as much as a 150-ton (136 t) blue whale.

- 12 school buses
- 30 elephants
- 1,700 adult humans

Hank's
WOOF OF WISDOM!

Female blue whales are larger and heavier than males.

Giants in Every Way

As you would expect, the giant blue whale has many huge body parts.

A blue whale's heart is the size of a Mini Cooper car.

Mini Cooper car

Hank's WOOF OF WISDOM!

About 100 people could fit into a blue whale's mouth. Its tongue weighs as much as an elephant.

The tube-like arteries that carry blood from a blue whale's heart are large enough for a person to crawl through!

Grooves

The pleats, or grooves, on a blue whale's throat and belly expand, or stretch. They allow the whale to take in enormous gulps of water when it is feeding.

Life in the Ocean

Adult blue whales do not live in large groups. These whales spend their time in pairs or small groups. Often, adult whales live alone.

Blue whales cruise the oceans, swimming at about 12 miles per hour (19 km/h).

If a blue whale is frightened or feels danger is near, however, it can swim at up to 30 miles per hour (48 km/h).

Blue whales usually swim at depths no deeper than 100 feet (30 m). They can stay underwater for up to 20 minutes before coming to the surface for air.

A small group of blue whales

Blue Whale Talk

Blue whales have the animal kingdom's loudest voices. They make deep, rumbling noises that sound like groans and moans.

A blue whale can make sounds that reach a volume of up to 200 **decibels**. A normal human conversation is about 60 decibels. The noise of a jet engine can reach 120 decibels.

These scientists are studying a blue whale.

Scientists think that blue whale noises can travel hundreds of miles (km) underwater. This means blue whales may be able to **communicate** with each other across oceans.

What's on the Menu?

You might think that in order to grow so huge, blue whales would feast on other large animals. In fact, blue whales feed on creatures that are no bigger than jelly beans.

Blue whales eat tiny, shrimp-like animals called **krill**.

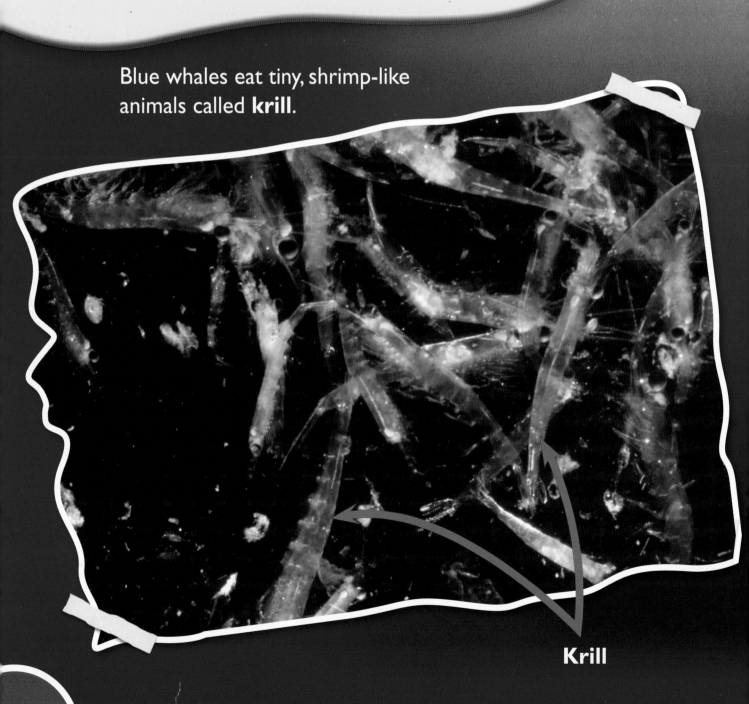

Krill

During times of the year when there are lots of krill in the ocean, a blue whale may eat 4 tons (3.6 t) of this food each day.

A swarm of krill

A blue whale feeding

A whale's 4-ton (3.6-t) meal of krill adds up to about 4 million individual tiny creatures!

Time to Feed

To eat 4 million krill in a day, a blue whale catches huge numbers of the little shellfish at one time.

A fringed baleen plate from a blue whale

Inside its mouth, a blue whale has stiff plates called baleen plates. These fringed plates grow down from the upper jaw and act like a strainer.

The whale gulps up a huge mouthful of water. It expands the grooves in its throat and belly to take in as much water as possible.

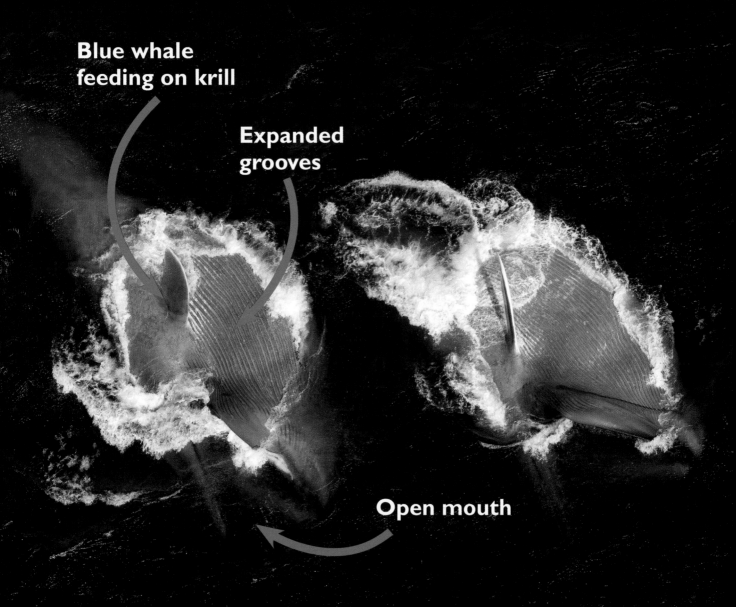

Blue whale feeding on krill

Expanded grooves

Open mouth

Next, the whale's huge tongue pushes the water back out of its mouth through its baleen plates. Tiny krill get trapped in the fringed baleen plates. Then the whale swallows the krill.

Meeting a Mate

When it is time to **mate**, adult male and female blue whales meet up.

Blue whales are ready to mate and have young when they are six to 10 years old. By this time, the whales have grown to about 70 to 80 feet (21–24 m) long.

Father blue whales do not help take care of their babies. After mating, a male and female blue whale couple leave each other.

**A pair of
blue whales**

Hank's
**WOOF OF
WISDOM!**

A female blue
whale is pregnant for
about 12 months.

A Giant Baby

A female blue whale gives birth to her calf underwater. The calf must soon swim to the surface to take its first breath.

When it is born, a blue whale is already 26 feet (8 m) long!

The newborn baby can weigh a super-heavy 4,500 pounds (2,000 kg.).

A blue whale calf feeds on milk from its mother's body. The baby whale drinks gallons (l) of rich, fatty milk each day.

Calf

Mother blue whale

Growing Fast

A blue whale calf's diet of fatty milk helps the baby grow bigger. It also helps the baby grow fast!

A blue whale calf gains about 200 pounds (91 kg) of weight each day. That's an incredible 8 pounds (3.6 kg) every hour!

A blue whale calf continues to drink milk until it is about eight months old. Then, like its mother, it feeds on krill.

Hank's
WOOF OF WISDOM!

Female blue whales have a calf every two to three years.

This blue whale is only a calf, but it's huge compared to a human.

In time, the youngster will leave its mother and begin its grown-up life.

Blue Whales in Danger

Blue whales were once hunted by humans for their fat, called blubber. Whale blubber was melted down to make oil for heating and lighting.

In the late 1800s and early 1900s, humans hunted blue whales until the animals were nearly **extinct.**

Finally, in 1966, the hunting of blue whales was banned around the world.

The numbers of blue whales have risen since the days of hunting, but only slowly.

There are still only 5,000 to 12,000 blue whales on Earth. Today, these beautiful ocean creatures are **endangered**.

Glossary

cetaceans (si-TAY-shunz) A group of animals that includes whales, dolphins, and porpoises. These animals are mammals that live in water.

communicate (kuh-MYOO-nih-kayt) To share facts or feelings.

decibels (DEH-sih-belz) Units of measurement used to measure how loud sounds are. Silence is measured as 0 decibels, while a gunshot is 140 decibels.

endangered (in-DAYN-jurd) In danger of no longer existing.

extinct (ek-STINGKT) No longer existing.

krill (KRIL) Tiny shrimp-like ocean animals with shells that are about the size of jelly beans.

mammals (MA-mulz) Warm-blooded animals that have a backbone, usually have hair, breathe air, and feed milk to their young.

mate (MAYT) When a male and female animal get together to produce young.

migrate (MY-grayt) To move to a new area for a period of time and then return. Animals may migrate to find food, to mate, or to avoid extreme weather.

streamlined (STREEM-lynd) Having a smooth and sometimes pointed shape that helps something move more quickly through the air or water.

Dr. Bob's Fast Fact Board

Compared to the rest of its body, a blue whale's eyes are quite small. Each eyeball is only about the size of a grapefruit.

Barnacles, small ocean creatures with shells, spend their lives attached to rocks and boats. Sometimes, they attach themselves to the tails and flippers of blue whales.

Blue whales live for about 90 years. The oldest blue whale ever found was believed to be about 110 years old!

People aren't allowed to hunt blue whales, but the animals are still in danger from humans. Blue whales are sometimes killed when they collide with boats. They can also be harmed by chemicals and other pollution in the ocean.

Websites

For web resources related to the subject of this book, go to:

www.windmillbooks.com/weblinks

and select this book's title.

Read More

Miller, Sara Swan. *Whales of the Arctic*. Brrr! Polar Animals. New York: PowerKids Press, 2009.

Parker, Steve. *Whales and Dolphins*. I Love Animals. New York: Windmill Books, 2011.

Rake, Jody Sullivan. *Blue Whales Up Close*. Whales and Dolphins Up Close. Mankato, MN: Capstone Press, 2010.

Index